Guyana

by Lisa Ally

Consultant: Marjorie Faulstich Orellana, PhD
Professor of Urban Schooling
University of California, Los Angeles

BEARPORT
PUBLISHING

New York, New York

Credits

Cover, © Stockyimages/Dreamstime and © Gail Johnson/Dreamstime; TOC, © Lev Kropotov/Shutterstock; 4, © BillH/iStock; 5T, © Wang LiQiang/Shutterstock; 5B, © Keren Su/China Span/Alamy; 7, © benedek/iStock; 8, © Gustavo Frazao/Shutterstock; 9, © Marcelo Alex/Shutterstock; 10, © Pete Oxford/Nature Picture Library/Alamy; 11, © Overflightstock Ltd/Alamy; 12T, © PhotocechCZ/Shutterstock; 12B, © Natalia Kuzmina/Shutterstock; 13T, © Paul R. Sterry/Nature Photographers Ltd/Alamy; 13B, © Lukas Blazek/Dreamstime; 14, © Creative Photo Corner/Shutterstock; 15, © Pictoral Press Ltd/Alamy; 16, © imageBROKER/Alamy; 17T, © benedek/iStock; 17B, © benedek/iStock; 18, © Natalia Gomyakova/Shutterstock; 19, © Heiner Heine/imageBROKER/AGE Fotostock; 20L, © Pacific Press/Sipa USA/Newscom; 20–21, © Zuma Press, Inc./Alamy; 22, © Maria_Lapina/iStock; 23T, © Ricky Soni Creations/Shutterstock; 23B, © nine_far/Shutterstock; 24–25, © wavebreakmedia/Shutterstock; 25R, © Molotok289/Shutterstock; 26, © Heiner Heine/imageBROKER/Alamy; 27, © Heritage Image Partnership Ltd/Alamy; 28, © Will Meinderts/BB/Minden Pictures/AGE Fotostock; 29, © Brian Overcast/Alamy; 30T, © Anton_Ivanov/Shutterstock and © Ermak Oksana/Shutterstock; 30B, © Gaardman/iStock; 31 (T to B), © Gail Johnson/Shutterstock, © Creative Photo Corner/Shutterstock, © Ammit Jack/Shutterstock, © Panya_Anakotmankong/Shutterstock, and © Chang W. Lee/The New York Times/Redux Pictures; 32, © Solodov Aleksei/Shutterstock.

Publisher: Kenn Goin
Senior Editor: Joyce Tavolacci
Creative Director: Spencer Brinker
Design: Debrah Kaiser
Photo Researcher: Thomas Persano

Library of Congress Cataloging-in-Publication Data

Names: Ally, Lisa, author.
Title: Guyana / by Lisa Ally.
Description: New York, New York : Bearport Publishing, [2019] | Series:
    Countries we come from | Includes bibliographical references and index.
Identifiers: LCCN 2018044185 (print) | LCCN 2018044315 (ebook) | ISBN
    9781642802610 (ebook) | ISBN 9781642801927 (library)
Subjects: LCSH: Guyana—Juvenile literature.
Classification: LCC F2368.5 (ebook) | LCC F2368.5 .A55 2019 (print) | DDC
    988.1—dc23
LC record available at https://lccn.loc.gov/2018044185

For more information, write to Bearport Publishing Company, Inc., 45 West 21st Street, Suite 3B, New York, New York 10010. Printed in the United States of America.

10 9 8 7 6 5 4 3 2 1

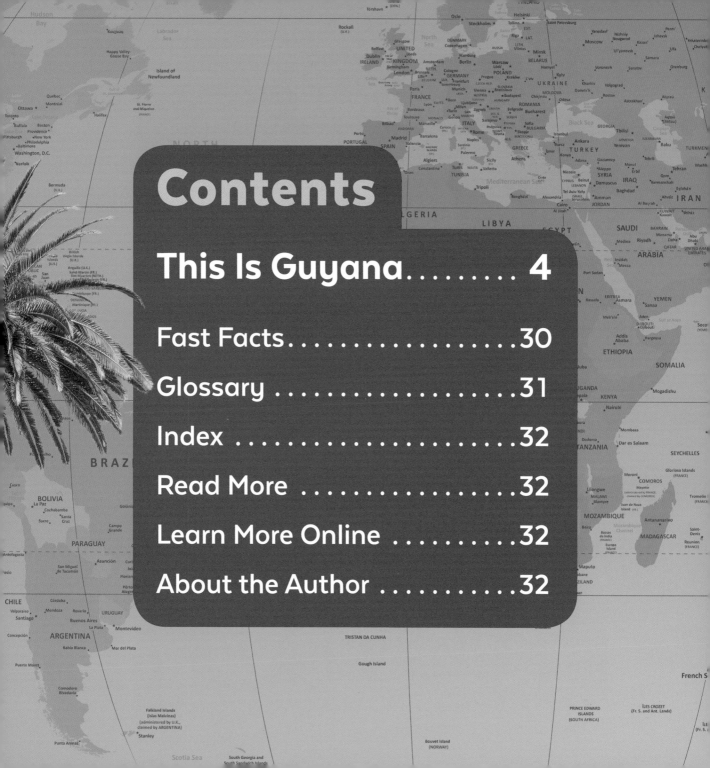

Contents

This Is Guyana

TROPICAL

WILD

Lively

Welcome to Guyana (guy-AN-uh)!

Guyana is a small country in South America.

About 700,000 people live there.

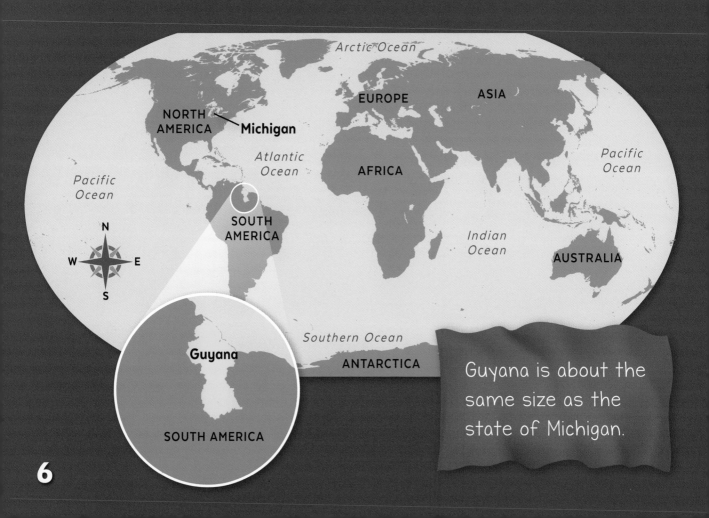

Guyana is about the same size as the state of Michigan.

Most of Guyana is covered with lush forests.

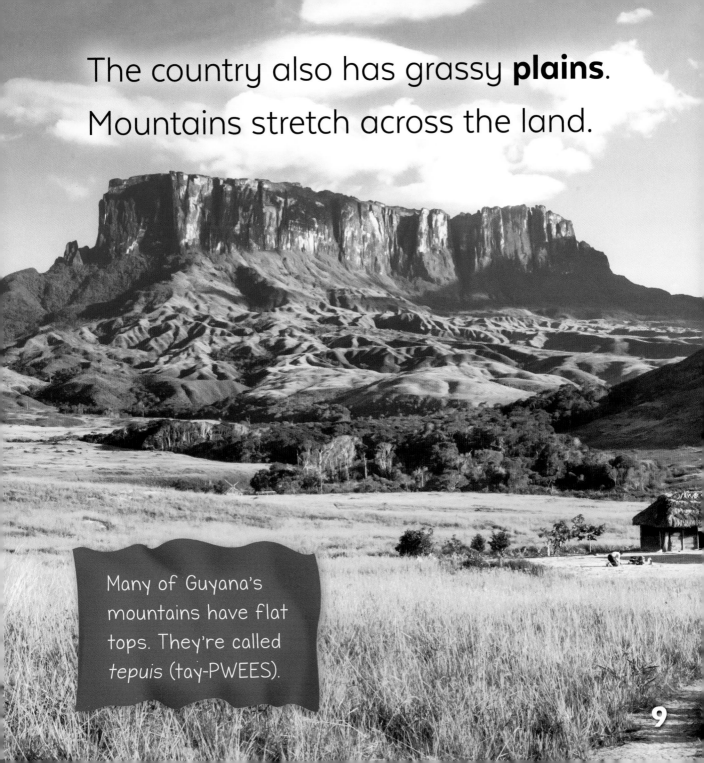

The country also has grassy **plains**. Mountains stretch across the land.

Many of Guyana's mountains have flat tops. They're called *tepuis* (tay-PWEES).

Over 50 rivers wind through the country.

The Essequibo River is the longest.

Guyana comes from a Native American word. It means "Land of Many Waters."

Many of the rivers form huge waterfalls. Guyana's Kaieteur Falls is four times taller than Niagara Falls!

Kaieteur Falls

Amazing animals live in Guyana's forests.

Giant otters splash into rivers.

Huge snakes slither on branches.

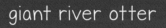
giant river otter

boa constrictor

Colorful birds
fly in the sky.

scarlet
ibises

Guyana's largest land
mammal is the tapir.

Guyana has a long history.

The Dutch and British ruled for hundreds of years.

They brought slaves from Africa to work the land.

In 1838, slavery was banned.

Guyana became a free country in 1966.

After 1838, the British brought workers from India to Guyana. The workers were treated almost as badly as slaves.

The **capital** of Guyana is Georgetown. It's also the country's largest city.

Georgetown is home to colorful Stabroek Market.

Shoppers can buy fruit, clothes, and other things there.

The market is known for its giant clock.

The main language in Guyana is English.

People also speak Creole, Hindi, and Urdu.

This is how you say *hello* in Creole:

Bonjou
(bawn-ZHOO)

This is how you say *hello* in Hindi:

Namaste
(nah-muh-STAY)

Guyana is the only English-speaking country in South America.

19

It's time to have fun!

The Mashramani Festival celebrates Guyana's **independence**.

People dress in colorful costumes.

There's a big parade.

The Mashramani Festival is held on February 23.

Guyanese food is spicy and flavorful.
Pepperpot is a sweet and spicy
meat stew.

Flat bread called roti is often eaten with it.

People in Guyana eat a lot of fruit. Carambola is a tasty star-shaped fruit!

What's the most popular sport in Guyana?

Cricket!

Cricket is similar to baseball.

The players whack a ball with a flat bat.

cricket bat

Guyana was the host of the 2007 Cricket World Cup.

Guyanese music is **unique**.

It includes African and Indian sounds.

People dance to the lively music!

Guyanese musicians often play guitars and drums.

Summer is a special time.
Hundreds of sea turtles come
to Guyana's Shell Beach.

They lay their eggs in the sand.

Weeks later, the babies hatch!
They crawl into the sea.

Four kinds of
sea turtles nest
on Shell Beach.

Fast Facts

Capital city: Georgetown

Population of Guyana: Over 700,000

Main language: English

Money: Guyanese dollar

Major religions: Christianity, Hinduism, and Islam

Neighboring countries: Brazil, Suriname, and Venezuela

Cool Fact: The national bird of Guyana is the blue-faced hoatzin (WHAT-sin). Chicks have claws on their wings to help them climb trees!

capital (KAP-uh-tuhl) the city where a country's government is based

independence (in-di-PEN-duhns) freedom from outside control

mammal (MAM-uhl) a warm-blooded animal that has hair or fur and drinks its mother's milk as a baby

plains (PLAYNZ) large, flat areas of land

unique (yoo-NEEK) one of a kind

Index

Read More

Morrison, Marion. *Guyana (Enchantment of the World).* New York: Children's Press (2003).

Temple, Bob. *Guyana (South America Today).* Broomall, PA: Mason Crest (2015).

Learn More Online

To learn more about Guyana, visit
www.bearportpublishing.com/CountriesWeComeFrom

About the Author

Lisa Ally is of Guyanese heritage and lives in Brooklyn, New York. She hopes to become a human rights attorney one day. She would like to dedicate this book to her mother, Susie, who taught her everything she knows.